THE MIRACLE LIFE SERIES

Your New Start

How to Begin Again

[signature: Melissa Flores]
Eph 4:24

International Standard Book Number
978-1-60458-856-9

Published by Valor House Publishing
301.895.3292
www.valorhousepublishing.com

Unless otherwise stated, all scripture
references are taken from the Holy Bible,
King James Version.

Table of Contents

4

Chapter 1

Where to Begin?

"Forget the former things; do not dwell on the past."
Isaiah 43:18

*"Your present circumstances don't determine where you
can go; they merely determine where you start."*
Nido Qubein

Every new start has a past. There is a sentence
before any period, a story before "the end." No
doubt, your new beginning has come on the heels
of a life-altering event. Whether it was the end of
a season, a choice or a tragedy that brought you
to this new start – *God is with you.*

He has said, *"Never will I leave you; never will I
forsake you,"* Hebrews 13:5 NIV. He did not leave
you when your former season came to a close and
He most certainly won't forsake you as your new
season begins. Ultimately, this new start is a gift
from God. Let us lay aside any question that
would hinder the opening of this gift. Put to rest
the urge to blame others, God or yourself for any
difficulty that has happened. Some find it easier

to blame, than to accept the responsibility of a new beginning. Simply acknowledge that in this life you may never know:

- Why it fell apart.
- How did this happen?
- Who was responsible?
- Where did things go wrong?
- When was the end apparent?
- What does it all mean?

Some answers come with time while others are reserved for us in Heaven. Only our Heavenly Father fully sees and understands all things. We can trust that He will, one day, reveal the answers to all of our questions. Until then, we must have faith in His ability to work out all things for our good (Romans 8:28).

Realize that God is fully committed to seeing you grow into the fullness of the character of Christ. This process is not delayed because of disappointments and setbacks. Rather, maturity is facilitated by hardship.

"Although Jesus was the Son [of God], he learned to be obedient through his sufferings," Hebrews 5:8 GWT.

You have been given the gift of a fresh start. At this point, it makes little difference what once was, what could have been, or what might have been. Now, only one thing is worth considering. *What will you do with your new beginning?* Do not let fear or regret hinder you from taking the most important steps of your life. Beginning again requires *faith — and faith comes by hearing good news.*

Remember, you are not the first person to start again. Scripture and history are replete with men and women who were devastated, only to find triumph after starting all over. As we examine a few of those stories, you'll be inspired to lay hold of the bright future God is making available to you. "*For I know the plans I have for you, declares the LORD, plans for welfare and not for evil, to give you a future and a hope,*" Jeremiah 29:11 ESV.

Processing the Past

There is a vast difference between dwelling on the past and addressing it. To "dwell" suggests that one "lives" out of the hurt of the past, or operates from a place of woundedness. Such a one feels persistent emotional pain and is not released to fully enjoy present living.

I once spoke with a dear man in his forties. He shared with me how his wife had taken everything he owned in a bitter divorce. The anger was palpable in his voice, *over fourteen years after the fact.* Another woman shared how as a teen, she had been abused by an older man in her family. Now, decades later, she continues to mistrust men, creating barriers to closeness with friends and potential spouses. One man shared with me how a former employer mistreated him during his tenure, eight years prior. His fists were angrily balled up as he described having to work long hours without overtime pay, among other expectations he fulfilled without reward. He vowed, in that conversation that he would never again allow himself to be taken advantage of.

Each of these individuals was unduly mistreated, creating a hurtful wound in the soul. Their emotions revealed that their wounds had not yet been addressed. Any unaddressed wound will continue to ache sorely and create a constant expectation of hurt in relationships or new endeavors.

Emotional wounds must be acknowledged and addressed else infection will eventually spread to every area of life. Unresolved issues have a way of poisoning fresh starts. Let us address any injury with a simple four-step plan to process the past.

1. Permit

Permit yourself to feel any loss, pain, hurt, disappointment, or anger. Be quick to admit, "This hurts!" In an attempt to be positive, strong, or spiritual, many refuse to acknowledge their own feelings in the midst of difficulty. Some place a higher premium on survival than dealing. <u>To deny there is pain is to enter into denial</u>. Simply defined, denial is the unwillingness or inability to fully acknowledge a situation and its consequences. Denial only delays the admission of hurt and suspends healing, further complicating the recovery process.

Loss of any kind will bring some level of grief to a healthy soul. Friend, God is not disappointed in us whenever we feel pain. He created us to share in His likeness by giving us the capacity to experience love, joy, peace, and even grief. Father identifies with us in our agony and draws us ever close to His heart.

Jesus taught us in Matthew 5:4, "*Blessed are they that mourn: for they shall be comforted.*" Those who are willing to mourn the past will receive the healing our Heavenly Father offers us. Those who refuse to admit there is anything to mourn, miss out on the comfort Heaven has to give. Pain has a purpose. To deny pain is to abort the process of being conformed into the image of His dear Son, *who also suffered for our sakes*. Suffering is an opportunity to enter into deeper fellowship with Christ. He has suffered more than we all. Any pain we deny is buried in our hearts, and further embedded deep within. Unaddressed

9

wounds will affect one's temperament, personality, and expectations for the future.

2. Pardon

Pardoning others releases us from the past. Keeping score sidelines us. The presence of blame is evidence that forgiveness has not been perfected in us. Once we release others and silence all talk of blame, we are free to view the offending party with accuracy and compassion.

Jesus said in Matthew 6:14 NIV, "*For if you forgive men when they sin against you, your heavenly Father will also forgive you.*" If we want God to go with us, we must be willing to release the guilty. This may include releasing *yourself*. Maybe you failed, played the fool, or even permitted someone else to do wrong. The weight of guilt will keep you from reaching your potential in life. Please do not punish yourself any longer. It serves no purpose since Jesus has already paid the price for your sin! Lay your guilt at the foot of His cross and enter into your destiny with Christ.

3. Ponder

"*Ponder the path of your feet, and let all your ways be established,*" Proverbs 4:26. We *can* and *should* learn *something* from *every* situation. Those who do not ponder their path are doomed to wander, repeating the same mistakes. Ask yourself, "What have I learned from the prior season?" "What will I do differently from here forward?" If you are having difficulty making sense of the situation, seek out counsel. A godly friend, pastor, prayer warrior, or counselor can help you see things from a higher perspective.

4. Picture

"*Let your eyes look straight ahead, fix your gaze directly before you.*" Proverbs 4:24 NIV. Allow the Spirit of God to stimulate your holy imagination. He wants to imprint your heart with a picture for your future. Perhaps, you have faithfully carried a picture that now seems impossible. Remember, "*For God's gifts and His call can never be withdrawn,*" Romans 11:29 NLT.

Routes may change and paths may cross, but your destination still waits. Do not be afraid to look at the future with the eyes of your heart. When your head makes decisions, it confers with your past. The heart, however, always consults your destiny when choosing its way. Rest assured, there is a way to *there* from *here*. Your heart with Christ enthroned is fit to lead the way.

Chapter 2

Financial Restarts

*"For though a righteous man falls
seven times, he rises again."*
Proverbs 24:16

*"The real measure of your wealth is how much you'd be
worth if you lost all your money."*
Anonymous

A surprising number of Americans are experiencing financial reversals of immense proportions. As of the printing of this book, 4.1% of all mortgages in the U.S. are in foreclosure.[1] Nearly 3 million homes have been lost since the housing crash of 2007. According to the Center for Responsible Lending, there are 6,600 new foreclosures daily, or one every 13 seconds.[2] Indications suggest the current crisis in the housing sector is far from over.

The American Bankruptcy Institute reports that 1,536,799 American citizens filed for bankruptcy in 2010.[3] Not every bankruptcy is the result of poor financial choices. According to Mark P.

Cussen of Investopedia.com, there are five common causes for personal bankruptcies in the U.S.[+]

1. **Medical Expenses.** A staggering 62% of all personal bankruptcies are the result of medical expenses. Interestingly, 78% of filers had some form of insurance. Being insured does not guarantee protection against bankruptcy.

2. **Job loss.** Losing one's job or becoming underemployed is the second leading cause of bankruptcy in the U.S. Many are released from work with little or no notice. Without severance pay, or an emergency fund, credit cards are often used to pay basic bills. If unemployment persists, this situation becomes increasingly difficult to overcome.

3. **Poor or excess use of credit.** The inability to control spending will eventually lead to the inability to make minimum payments to creditors. If debt consolidation loans cannot be obtained, the borrower has no choice but to file for bankruptcy.

4. **Divorce or separation.** Separation puts intense financial strain on families. The resources that sustained one household are now divided to maintain two. Legal fees, alimony, and/or child support can be the proverbial straw that breaks the camel's back.

5. **Unexpected Expenses.** Loss of home and possessions due to unexpected disasters or tragedies can send people over the brink of insolvency. Some have lost their livelihoods due to an illness or family situation.

While bankruptcy is growing more common, it is not completely unavoidable. There are options worth first, considering.

1. **Debt consolidation.** This is the process of combining smaller debts into one larger payment. (Example: combining balances on higher interest or variable interest credit cards into one account with a fixed lower interest rate.) Personal loans or home equity loans can be obtained for the same purpose. This is only effective if the interest rate of the *new* loan is significantly lower. This can help to lower the amount of money being made

14

monthly to payments. Caution! This relief can tempt the consumer to make further debt, worsening the situation.

2. **Financial planning**. There are professionals who are skilled in helping you make the most of your resources. With their help, you can discover your true financial status, establish goals, develop a plan, and make the necessary lifestyle adjustments to achieve that plan. Crown Financial Ministries is a non-profit faith-based organization that has helped millions with financial planning. They can be found online at www.crown.org.

3. **Credit counselor**. A credit counseling agency will help consumers pay off debt by negotiating reduced interest rates with one's creditors. This lowers monthly payments to a more manageable sum. Using a credit counseling agency means one must agree <u>not</u> to open new credit or use existing credit accounts while involved in the program. Before using a credit-counseling agency, investigate its reputability. One of the most highly recommended is the non-profit organization, Clearpoint Credit

Counseling Services (formerly known as Consumer Credit Counseling Services). They can be found online at www.cccsstl.org

Many have lost everything to start all over again. These successful people found prosperity after having declared bankruptcy: Milton Hershey, founder of Hershey's Chocolate; Henry Ford, founder of Ford Motors; Walt Disney, creator of Mickey Mouse; Donald Trump, real estate tycoon; J.J. Heinz, ketchup mogul; and Abraham Lincoln, businessman turned politician. Financial reversals do not have to be the end of your dreams for prosperity. Many who have started over have remarked about the great peace that came after placing their future into the hands of God. True prosperity begins with prosperity of spirit and soul. Allow God to wipe away any disappointment or shame. Once healing comes to the heart, material blessings naturally follow.

Believe for Miracles

One must never rule out the miraculous. In 2 Kings 4, we read of a widow whose deceased husband left her and their two sons in a world of debt. Without an income, the family could not meet their financial obligations. The creditor, by legal right, was about to claim the two boys as slaves. Otherwise hopeless, the widow sought the help of Elisha, the prophet. He answered the woman in 2 Kings 4:2 NIV, "*How can I help you? Tell me, what do you have in your house?*"

The woman answered, "*Your servant has nothing there at all, except a little oil.*"

Elisha commanded her in verses 3 and 4, "*Go around and ask all your neighbors for empty jars. Don't ask for just a few. Then go inside and shut the door behind you and your sons. Pour oil into all the jars, and as each is filled, put it to one side.*"

The widow and her sons did as they were told, and every jar was filled until there weren't any jars left. The prophet then said in verse 7, "*Go, sell the oil and pay your debts. You and your sons can live on what is left.*"

Never underestimate what Heaven can do in destitute situations. The Lord has been known to take up the cause of the fatherless and the widow. Our Heavenly Father is most charitable! Let us take three cues from the widow who obtained her miracle by faith.

1. **Seek divine assistance.** The widow sought advice from the Lord, through the prophet. Be sure to pray about your situation. Consult the Word of God for pertinent scriptures that will instruct

you in financial righteousness. For every problem, there is a biblical principle that can bring deliverance.

2. **Work with what you have.** Elisha did not focus on what the woman lacked, rather what she *had*. As little as it was, the oil mixed with faith was enough to fuel a financial miracle of epic proportions.

3. **Shut the doors.** By shutting the doors, the widow and her sons were closing out potential distraction. Let nothing divert your focus as you follow the Lord's leading to financial breakthrough.

Importantly, the widow did not receive a heavenly handout. She and her sons had to work in obedience to the word they were given. Every vessel had their fingerprints - every drop of oil poured by their hands. Freely offer the Lord whatever resources you may have, in faith believing, and see what He will do.

Scriptures for further encouragement:

"Owe no one anything, except to love each other, for the one who loves another has fulfilled the law."
Romans 13:8 NLT

"It is better that you should not vow than that you should vow and not pay."
Ecclesiastes 5:5 ESV

"And you shall hallow the fiftieth year and you shall proclaim liberty throughout the land to all its inhabitants. It shall be a jubilee for you: you shall return, every one of you, to your property and every one of you to your family."
Leviticus 25:10 KJV

"The Spirit of the Lord is upon me, because he has anointed me to bring good news to the poor. He has sent me to proclaim release to the captives and recovery of sight to the blind, to let the oppressed go free."
Luke 4:18 KVJ

Chapter 3

New Career

*"That everyone may eat and drink, and find satisfaction
in all his toil, this is the gift of God."*
Ecclesiastes 3:13

"If opportunity doesn't knock, build a door."
Milton Berle

If you have found yourself unemployed or
underemployed, you are not alone. A Gallup
report[1] released at the close of 2011 found
underemployment in the United States (without
seasonal adjustment) to be at 18.4%. This figure
includes those who are unemployed as well as
those who are working part-time but desire full-
time labor. Just over 18% of American workers
are not bringing home the income they feel is
necessary for a satisfactory standard of living.

The unemployment office is filled with educated,
experienced, and qualified people who have been
victimized by the recent changes in our economy.
The facts of our times, however, cannot negate
the truth of God's Word! God is capable of

turning any misfortune into an opportunity for
your advancement.

Unjust Dismissal

Consider Joseph. In Genesis 37, we read how
Joseph was Jacob's favorite son. The favor of his
father invoked the persecution of his brothers. To
be rid of him, his brothers sold him as a slave to
Ishmaelite traders. Two chapters later, we find
Joseph performing as an exemplary slave in the
household of Potiphar. He developed great skill
in running Potiphar's affairs. "*From the time he put
him in charge of his household and of all that he
owned, the Lord blessed the household of the Egyptian
because of Joseph. The blessing of the Lord was on
everything Potiphar had, both in the house and in the
field*," Genesis 39:5.

God blessed everything Joseph touched.
Heaven's blessings, however, could not save him
in the day of false accusation. His unwillingness
to succumb to the sexual advances of Potiphar's
wife set him up for retaliation. Furious at being
declined, she erased any memory of his
faithfulness with vindictive lies.

Subsequently, Joseph was fired *and* imprisoned.

The blessing of God followed him into the
prison, where his skills were eventually

employed, again. Albeit a different job and location, the same anointing brought him to a place of management and success. Through a series of events, Joseph (who was also an interpreter of dreams) was eventually brought before Pharaoh.

Pharaoh had two troubling dreams that could not be interpreted. No one else could discern the meaning of his dreams. This, of course, was a divine setup by God, who had given Joseph the gifts of interpretation and wisdom. Joseph's gift created a door for him in Pharaoh's court. Thanks to this imprisoned slave, the nation would now be spared a horrendous downfall due to the coming famine described in the king's dream.

In the end, Pharaoh employed Joseph. Second in command of a world empire, Joseph was put in position to use all the skills he had acquired during years of unjust hardship. He would one day be reunited with his brothers and tell them, "*You intended to harm me, but God intended it for good to accomplish what is now being done, the saving of many lives,*" Genesis 50:20 NIV.

No false accusation has the power to undo the call of God on your life. If you have been unjustly dismissed, the Lord now has the opportunity to move you closer to your destiny. The gifts Father has given you are creating and opening doors for you, even now.

Stuck in a Rut

Consider Elisha. In 1 Kings 19:19, we find this man contently plowing in his family field. The comfort of working the family farm was soon to be challenged by the prophet, Elijah. As he plowed behind twelve yoke of oxen, Elijah passed by and threw his mantle around him. The choice was made in an instant. "Do I continue plowing these ruts?" or "Do I follow Elisha into an unknown future?"

The call of the prophet resonated deeply within the heart of Elisha. In order to leave the ruts, he daringly slaughtered his oxen and burned his plow. After the meat was given to people, he set out to follow his new career.

Maybe you have been stuck in a rut that pays the bills, but leaves the heart longing. Your Elijah might be the calling of God to embrace a new career or ministry. Be prepared to burn the plow and cook the oxen. Great exploits are in your future!

Awaiting Open Doors

Regardless if your employment situation is through your fault, false accusation, or by no fault of your own… *Father has a plan.* There is forgiveness for mistakes, and restoration for losses and hope for future success. It is His desire that all of His children prosper in their land. Deuteronomy 8:8 promises the righteous, "*The Lord will send a blessing on your barns and on everything you put your hand to. The Lord your God will bless you in the land He is giving you.*"

Assess what doors have closed and which are opening. In the ever-increasing Kingdom of God, no door closes without another one opening. Though you might feel helpless, Father is already looking to your future. "*See, I have placed before you an open door that no one can shut. I know that you have little strength, yet you have kept my word and have not denied my name,*" Revelation 3:8 NIV.

If no door seems to be opening, look in a different direction. It may be time to entertain a new career path or a return to school. It's never too late to obtain or complete a degree. According to the National Center for Higher Education Management Systems, 40% of the nation's college and university students are 25 years of age or older[2]. The Council for Adult and Experiential Learning reported in 2004 that adult learners made up nearly 43% of enrollment in community colleges[3]. Many are taking advantage of their current circumstances to acquire an education or new skills.

Your experience will not be wasted. God is able to recycle your skills wherever He sends you, next. Flexibility is critical during seasons of change. The one who gains identity from his job or pay-grade will have a more difficult time transitioning to a new assignment. Adapting comes more easily to the one who is willing to trust the Lord with his future. You must be willing to burn your plow!

Finally, any open door must be walked through. Have the courage to step into the unknown. What do you have to lose? No doubt, there are dreams and goals within your heart that have yet to be realized. The choice you make, today, could launch you into your destiny!

Scriptures for further encouragement:

"Don't worry about anything; instead, pray about everything. Tell God what you need, and thank Him for all He has done."
Phillipians 4:6 NLT

"And why do you worry about clothes? See how the lillies of the field grow. They do not labor or spin."
Matthew 6:28 NIV

"We wait in hope for the Lord; He is our help and shield." Psalm 33:20 NIV

"Sustain me according to Your word, that I may live; And do not let me be ashamed of my hope."
Psalm 119:116 NASB

"In Him we were also chosen, having been predestined according to the plan of Him who works out everything in conformity with the purpose of His will."
Ephesians 1:11 NIV

Chapter 4

Relocating

*"The righteous keep moving forward, and those with
clean hands become stronger and stronger."*
Job 17:9 NLT

"For every problem there is an opportunity."
Anonymous

Boxes. Newspaper. Packing tape. Moving truck
& blankets. Mail-forwarding request. Utilities
transfer. *Check.* If only moving was as easy as
packing – lifting – traveling – lifting - unpacking!
There are a hundreds of considerations that
culminate in the ultimate choice to relocate.
Because of the financial cost and stress involved,
moving is generally considered a life-changing
event – *a new beginning*.

One in six Americans will relocate to a different
home this year.[1] In times past, people moved only
rarely. Retirement-aged Americans have lived
statistically in an average of 5 homes. Today's
typical American will relocate 11.7 times in a
lifetime.[2] Certain cultural developments have

contributed to the trend of relocating every five to seven years. Here are ten common reasons why people relocate:

1. **Occupational change.** Many move to find work or are transferred by their employer.
2. **Outgrowing home.** As families grow, more room is often necessary.
3. **Death.** When a loved one dies, it is sometimes easier to leave a home full of memories. The loss of a spouse may also leave one financially incapable of maintaining the existing home and/or mortgage.
4. **Empty Nest/Retirement.** When children leave, a smaller home may be more sensible. Many retirement-age Americans are opting for simpler living. Active adult communities have become increasingly popular, providing community and safety.
5. **Family.** Many prefer to live near family to promote togetherness, share resources, or to help give care for the elderly.
6. **Divorce.** At least one partner will need to relocate during a separation and divorce. Sometimes both partners will relocate to liquidate the home.
7. **Turning a new leaf.** Some relocate to a new city when making a break with the past. It is sometimes necessary to completely abandon a dangerous or toxic environment.

8. **Flipping.** Enterprising handy-folks enjoy buying homes they can remodel and sell for profit. This can be a very gratifying way to use one's skills for profit.

9. **Liquidating.** Homes with equity are a great source of cash in times of need. Others are forced to move because of financial setbacks.

10. **Health.** Declining health can make it difficult to maintain a home. Some find it necessary to relocate to easier or rented environs.

Some new seasons require a change of address. There are times whenever fidelity to God might require a move from an unsavory situation. A number of years ago, a young couple accepted Christ in our church. These two precious people had co-habited before meeting Jesus. Autonomously, they decided after conversion, that one had to move out – until they married. Honor was granted to their relationship with this decision to respect biblical principle.

Another gentleman came back to the Lord after years of living a homosexual lifestyle. He found it necessary to completely abandon the city he was living in, to break emotional ties with the faces and places in his past. His fresh start necessitated new scenery. Geography stimulates memories that can easily pull one back into former sin habits. This man made a successful break with the homosexual lifestyle because of his willingness to start all over again.

One young couple had difficulty in the early years of marriage because of overbearing in-laws. Living close by, the two were expected to be at his mom's dinner table several times a week. As you might imagine, this did not go over well with the young bride who desperately wanted to set up housekeeping for her groom. After many months of failing to establish healthy boundaries, the young couple decided to relocate a couple dozen miles away. The distance was just enough to create a healthy boundary for the relieved couple. Great peace ensued.

Obeying God

In scriptural record, there are a number of people who had no choice but to relocate. Abraham heard the voice of God in Genesis 12:1-2 NIV. *"Leave your country, your people and your father's household and go to the land I will show you. I will make your name great, and you will be a blessing."* Abraham willingly moved to step into the blessing that awaited him in a new land. His choice to relocate placed him in the center of God's will.

Fleeing Trouble

In Matthew 2:13 NIV, Joseph, Mary and Jesus were commanded to flee their home because of the threat of Herod. An angel appeared to Joseph in a dream and said, "*'Get up, take the child and his mother and escape to Egypt. Stay there until I tell you, for Herod is going to search for the child to kill him.'*" Jesus, Joseph and Mary stayed in Egypt for an extended period of time until the danger had subsided. Imagine the culture shock that awaited them in the idolatrous society of Egypt! Father God ordained this time, however, for the preservation of the Messiah.

Hearing God is the key to a successful relocation. You may be transplanted into a less-than-desirable situation, *for a season*. Knowing God is with you, in your move, makes it possible to endure great difficulties. Here are some simple questions to take to the Lord, whenever weighing any relocation.

1. ***Will this move take me closer to or further from my God-given destiny?*** Precious years can be lost with just one misstep. Be certain you are following the compass of your high call in Christ Jesus.

2. *Will this move contribute to my emotional and spiritual stability, and that of my family?* Uprooting children from their school, friends, and church greatly impacts their emotional wellbeing. Adults also struggle with having to build new relationships from the ground up. If a move is God-ordained, however, there will be great grace to ease the burden. Also worth considering, a move might be necessary to help the family make a break with destructive relationships. In this case, a move could be a large leap *toward* emotional stability.

3. *Is there a bible-teaching, spirit-filled church where I desire to move?* Some choose to move for economic betterment. More money profits little, however, if the family is unplugged from the body of Christ. Don't let this move be the death of your family's faith.

4. *Are there covenant relationships in place where I'm heading?* How difficult it is to start over without having anyone familiar, nearby! Even more problematic is the absence of any covenant relationship. Covenant speaks of a spiritual bond or commitment between two parties that exists for

mutual benefit and encouragement. Is there someone in or near your perspective new town, who will be present in the best and worst of times?

5. **Am I moving to escape problems that I am unwilling to address?** Any problem we flee will find us in our future. Do everything in your power to heal, reconcile, or make things right, else the problem will resurface again in your new environment. Problems only vanish *after* being solved.

Scriptures for further encouragement:

"Thy word is a lamp unto my feet, and a light unto my path." Psalm 119:105 KJV

"Commit your works to the Lord and your plans will be established." Proverbs 16:3 NASB

"And he said to them all, 'If any man will come after me, let him deny himself, and take up his cross daily, and follow me.'" Luke 9:23 KJV

"God blessed them and said to them, 'Be fruitful and increase in number; fill the earth and subdue it.'" Genesis 1:28 NIV

"There is surely a future hope for you, and your hope will not be cut off." Proverbs 23:18 NIV

Chapter 5

Divorce

"Praise be to the God and Father of our Lord Jesus Christ, the Father of compassion and the God of all comfort, who comforts us in all our troubles."
2 Corinthians 1:3-4 NLT

"God is closest to those with broken hearts." Jewish Proverb

"I never should have left him." My friend laid the pieces of her broken heart on the kitchen table between us. "I don't really know why I left," she sobbed. "Now, it's over. Look at the mess I've made!"

It is possible for a marriage to break beyond repair. The pain of a shattered relationship can certainly break down one's will to work toward reconciliation. My friend could not pinpoint why her marriage had failed. According to H. Norman Wright, there are four generally unidentified reasons why husbands and wives walk away from their vows.[1]

1. *One or both persons fail to understand the stages and changes of individual development — the seasons of their lives — and how these affect their marriage.*[2] Women and men experience a transition in identity at critical times in their lives. Both genders see these changes happen at 30, and again near 40. Many divorces happen around these pivotal identity transitions.

2. *People have an inadequate basis upon which they build their personal identity and security.*[3] Outer beauty and personal performance can change and even fade with age and circumstance. If husband and/or wife fail to love one another unwaveringly through the maturation process, the marriage cannot survive.

3. *People come to marriage with either unresolved issues between themselves and their parents or they come from dysfunctional families, and this intrudes upon their marriage.*[4] Dysfunction must be addressed in premarital counseling. If pre-existing troubles follow the couple into marriage, the relationship can unravel around those very issues.

4. *Some marriages dissolve because the partners were never prepared for marriage and because their expectations about marriage were totally*

unrealistic.[5] People sometimes marry with ideas of unrealistic romanticism. Others leap into marriage because of societal or familial expectations, or the ticking biological clock. For many, marriage seems like the proper answer to loneliness, sexual desires, or even depression.

These four underlying reasons are generally the impetus for emotional withdrawal, relational breakdown, infidelity, or even abuse. Discovering the "why" is crucial to moving on in life.

Defeat Shame

Shame is the residue of divorce. Divorce makes one feel flawed, guilty, or even like a failure. These emotions can affect one's ability to properly heal. Heavenly Father does not correct His children with shame, but instead offers truth and grace. Know that God has stored up goodness for those who fear Him, and who take refuge in Him (Psalm 31:19). Run to the Lord with any shame and brokenness. He will help you discover the truth about your situation, and offer the grace needed to heal and move on. When understanding and grace enters, shame leaves.

If you have suffered a divorce, you are certainly not alone. According to the Barna Research Group[6], 11% of the adult U.S. population is currently divorced. Twenty-five percent of all adults have had at least one divorce. These statistics are virtually echoed within the walls of the church. Consequently, others who have shared similar grief surround you. Many have come to a place of wholeness, and you can too!

What Hinders Healing?

There are 7 traps to avoid as you work through a divorce.

1. **Not seeking legal help.** Promises made during a separation are rarely kept. Protect yourself and your family by gaining legal counsel.

2. **False expectations of your in-laws.** It is the exception, not the rule, that your in-laws will remain close after your divorce. Prepare your heart, as your in-laws will likely remain loyal to their blood relation.

3. **Schedule overload.** People can often cram far too much into their schedule to prevent alone time. This can sap much needed energy, both physically and

emotionally. Schedule overload is also a sign that the hurting individual is not yet ready to face the painful truth of their new reality.

4.   **Emotional detachment.** When we are overwhelmed with pain, it is natural to withdraw emotionally. If we are unable to release pain by admitting it, sharing it with others, and forgiving, we can shut down emotionally.

5.   **Self-focused attitude.** Because of the pain of rejection, one can turn his or her focus inward. This results in a fixation on bettering oneself, defending oneself, or indulging oneself.

6.   **Premature romantic relationships.** It is _never_ acceptable to foster a romantic relationship during a time of separation. It is _never_ appropriate to move into a relationship without having fully healed from the previous one. A new romance cannot heal you. It takes two to five years to heal properly from a broken marriage. The healing time depends largely on the individual and the circumstances surrounding the separation. Until you are whole and

happy living alone, *you are not ready to date*.

7. **Bonding with dysfunctional people.** Injured people look for others who share their pain. One can be inundated with unwanted advice. Watch for those seeking opportunity to unload their toxic pasts! Guard your heart and ears. The only ones qualified to help share your burden, are those who have walked where you have walked, and have emerged victorious. It is common to develop new friendships during a divorce. Don't choose the faithless, unbelieving and bitter.

4 Steps to Wholeness

If you are broken, *you will heal*. However, you want to heal properly and move on as a whole individual. Here are four steps to wholeness.

1. **Do self-maintenance.** Make sure you eat, exercise, rest, drink plenty of water, and all the things that promote physical health. These gestures will contribute to your emotional wellbeing, and exercise releases stress.

2. **Devote yourself.** Draw closer to God. He has orchestrated healing for you through His Word, His house, and His people. This is an opportune time to begin a prayer journal to express feelings, thoughts and prayers. Draw near to God and He will draw near to you (James 4:8).

3. **Discover yourself.** Many times our identities are skewed by our spouse's perception of us. A married couple, as husband and wife, will have an enmeshed identity. You will need to find out who you are as a single person. There is far more to you than being a spouse. Stretch beyond your comfort zone to explore new friendships and activities. Unearth former hopes, past ambitions, or even hobbies you have laid down or postponed. This new beginning can awaken dormant giftings and dreams within you.

4. **Develop yourself.** Prophesy your future by developing vision for the days ahead. Only a foolish person places his past in his future. Begin to declare new things over your life. Ask God to flood your life with new opportunities for growth and advancement. Set goals that

will bring you fulfillment and enrichment. You may choose to finish your degree, take a short-term missions trip, volunteer in a worthwhile organization, etc. Do something that restores your soul and lifts your spirit.

Scriptures for further encouragement:

"But if the husband or wife who isn't a believer insists on leaving, let them go. In such cases the Christian husband or wife is no longer bound to the other, for God has called you to live in peace."
1 Corinthians 7:15 NLT

"Get rid of all bitterness, rage and anger, brawling and slander, along with every form of malice. Be kind and compassionate to one another, forgiving each other, just as in Christ God forgave you."
Ephesians 4:31-32 NIV

"Let me hear of your unfailing love each morning, for I am trusting you. Show me where to walk, for I give myself to you." Psalm 13:8 NLT

"'But I will restore you to health and heal your wounds,' declares the Lord, 'because you are called an outcast, Zion for whom no one cares.' '...I will bring him near and he will come close to me, for who is he who will devote himself to be close to me?'"
Jeremiah 30:17 & 21 NIV

Rebuilding Estranged Relationships

"For this son of mine was dead and is alive again; he was lost and is found."
The Prodigal Father

Broken people produce broken relationships. Each relationship has a certain set of written or unwritten rules, which engenders love, safety and mutual respect. If that code is dishonored, trust is broken and communication falters. Relational breaches can be attributed to neglect, dishonor, or betrayal. In an ideal world, no relationship would ever be disrupted. Because of sin, however, every person will experience the bruise of a wrecked relationship. We must choose, then, whether or not to pursue reconciliation.

Our Heavenly Father is the Master Reconciliator. Before His most treasured creation, man, betrayed Him in the Garden, God had already crafted a plan for reconciliation. Jesus was, *"The Lamb was slain from the creation of the world,"* Revelation 13:8 NIV. The Bible is the unfolding of that beautiful plan. Jesus is the bridge Father built to span the breach between us.

We take our cue from His example. How many relationships in your past might have gone differently if your heart was pursuant to reconciliation? As God has demonstrated, someone has to build a bridge – or leave the door open for restoration. Be ready to face resistance or indifference from the estranged. Although you are ready to reconcile, he or she may not be. Patience is critical. Even though you may build a world-class bridge, you cannot force your friend or loved one to cross it. With prayer and diligence, however, your efforts may prove worthwhile.

Build a Bridge

Bridge building begins with seeking and/or giving forgiveness. If you share even partial responsibility for the breakdown, an apology is the first step. He or she will have difficulty moving beyond any unrepentant offense.

If the estranged is the perpetrator of the hurt, forgiveness must be granted before pursuing reconciliation. Accept that you may never get the apology you deserve. If you desire to rebuild a connection, release him or her from any guilt in the past. You might not know why the breakdown happened, if it was against your will. Understand that people abandon situations that they feel helpless to change, unable to accept, or handle. If this is the case, he or she may need time to regain control of emotions or arrive at a place of acceptance and stability.

Meanwhile, pray for your loved one. Ask Heaven to heal and mend his or her heart to the point where an attempt to reconnect will be successful.

Adjust Expectations

The story of the prodigal in Luke 15:11-31 gives us a picture of a successful reconnection between an estranged father and son. The younger of two sons asked for his inheritance early. Granting his request, the kindly father knew full well the son might squander every penny. During the time of estrangement, the son exhausted his inheritance on wild living. The Father, however, kept looking and waiting for the return of his lost boy. When the son finally came around, it is written in verse 20, *"His father saw him and was filled with compassion for him; he ran to his son, threw his arms around him and kissed him."* Imagine the horror of seeing this once strapping young lad, weakly tripping through the field, now emaciated and haggard! The father's heart leapt with compassion, immediately adjusting his expectations of the newfound son.

After a period of estrangement, you will need to adjust any expectations you may have of your loved one. The brokenness that separated you in the first place, will likely have manifested in other areas of his or her life. You may be surprised to find radical changes in his or her spiritual state. Addiction, financial ruin, sickness, depression, or any other difficulties may now be a part of his or her existence. Reunions of this sort rarely find both parties in the same condition as when they parted ways.

After long periods of estrangement, it can be even more painful to discover the lost one has moved on. You might reconnect only to discover your loved one has nurtured a family, job, and new relationships, apart from your involvement. Any previous expectations must be adjusted to accommodate the changes that have taken place.

Some have had to give up the expectation of being present at their child's wedding, or the birth of a grandchild. Others have had to give up the hope of seeing their son or daughter graduate college. Every estrangement will cause a disappointment of certain expectations. We must adapt if we are to wholeheartedly welcome back the lost one.

Freely Accept

In scripture, the prodigal father liberally lavished affection and open acceptance. On the evening of the boy's return, a great feast was served with music and dancing. It is quite acceptable to rejoice with others over your reconciliation – even if your loved one is still in need of healing and restoration. The father did not hide him away, until his health returned. Rather, he openly accepted the son *because of who he was*.

Love does not condone wrongdoing. If the returning one is unrepentant or entrenched in a sinful lifestyle, you may freely love without enabling or condoning. Go ahead and celebrate, but prepare to forge healthy boundaries.

Set Limitations

Re-establishing a relationship after a period of estrangement will be awkward. Both you and the returning one may need to create ground rules for proceeding. Certain behaviors may require that you limit your interaction or contact for the safety and wellbeing of you and your family. Reconciliation does not mean total acceptance of a problematic lifestyle. Tough love may be necessary to protect the innocent and to nurture true healing in the heart of the offender. Trust must again be cultivated, which requires time and testing.

Consider also, that much grace will be needed to dispel any fear of repeated rejection *within you. Perfect love casts out all fear.* Do not permit wrongdoing because of the fear of losing an opportunity. "*The righteousness of the upright will be their guide, but the twisted ways of the false will be their destruction,*"Proverbs 11:3.

The estranged may feel the need to limit interactions at first, until safety is established. Resist the urge to demand time, or to guilt your loved one into coming around more frequently. Do not be surprised if visits or phone calls are brief and uneventful, at first. Your gentleness and longsuffering will convince them of your authenticity. With gentle coaxing, guards come down. If not at first, in time your loved one may walk across the bridge you have built.

Do not lose hope of reconciliation with long lost loved ones. A father was contacted by his estranged daughter nearly 10 years after their relationship was wrecked. One short phone call broke a decade of silence, and opened the door to many subsequent conversations. He now enjoys meaningful visits with his geographically removed grandchildren several times a year. His prayers and patience paid off.

Scriptures for further encouragement:

"Bear with each other and forgive whatever grievances you may have against one another. Forgive as the Lord forgave you." Colossians 3:13 NIV

"All this is from God, who reconciled us to himself through Christ and gave us the ministry of reconciliation." 2 Corinthians 5:18 NIV

"So we are Christ's ambassadors; God is making his appeal through us. We speak for Christ when we plead, 'Come back to God!'" 2 Corinthians 5:20 NLT

"And he shall turn the heart of the fathers to the children, and the heart of the children to their fathers; lest I come and smite the earth with a curse." Malachi 4:6 ASV

"And, having made peace through the blood of his cross, by him to reconcile all things unto himself; by him, I say, whether they be things in earth, or things in heaven." Colossians 1:20 KVJ

Chapter 7

Death of a Loved One

"While we are mourning the loss of our friend, others are rejoicing to meet him behind the veil."
John Taylor

"Weeping may tarry for the night, but joy comes with the morning."
Psalm 30:5 ESV

The strongest medicine on earth cannot quench the pain of a grieving heart. The ones we cherish most leave imprints on our soul that time and separation cannot erase. This is the influence of love on the human heart. Overwhelming sorrow is to be expected as one comes to grips with the reality of his loss. Sorrow, however, gradually lessens as the heart learns to let go. Once we have released our loved one to his or her new beginning, *we are ready for our own.*

We have no choice but to begin again as our world is forever altered. The beloved can never be replaced. Happiness, on the other hand, can sprout again in the soil of the human heart.

Release is achieved whenever we overcome five common fears during the grieving season.

1. **Your feelings or lack of them are not wrong.** Some fear grieving too much, or too little. Everyone mourns differently. Also, expect intermittent periods of joy and sorrow as the mourning process progresses. Eventually, moments of deep sorrow will strike less and less often.

2. **You will not forget your loved one.** As the pain of loss decreases, one may fear also losing cherished memories. Photo albums, memorials and scrapbooks are great ways to keep memories alive.

3. **Your loved one would want you to move on.** Do not entertain imaginations that your spouse, child, family member or friend might be angry with you for putting your life back together. Those in the heavenly cloud of witnesses, now see life on this earth with new eyes.

4. **The plan God has for your life has not changed.** It may feel that "Plan A" has come to an end. The exceedingly

good plan God has for your life is not contingent upon who enters or exits. Our earthly roles may change as a result of a loved one's passing. The fullness of God's unchanging will, however, will be realized as we obediently follow Him through both blessing and heartbreak.

5. **Life will be good, again.** "*I believe that I will see the goodness of the Lord in this world of the living.*" Psalm 27:13 GWT. Make this your daily declaration.

A New Day

Patience is key when moving forward. After a few good days, weeks or even months, you may have a rough go of it. You may wonder, "How long will I hurt?" Experts suggest the first year is significantly challenging. It is never easy to cross all the milestones of birthdays, anniversaries, holidays, etc. You may find yourself slipping back into grief on or around these important dates. Do your best to prepare as you work to establish new traditions. As time progresses, the memory of your loved one will bring more joy than pain. Although we never "get over" the loss of someone we love, we can learn to carry memories with gladness and thanksgiving.

The final stage of grieving involves reinvesting oneself in other relationships. Feelings of guilt may arise as you do, however, this is a necessary step for healing.

Remarriage after the Death of a Spouse

If a spouse has passed away, it may be natural for the widow or widower to eventually long for companionship. While together in life, many make vows to never remarry should death claim their spouse. Nobody can predict how his or her heart will heal, or whether there will eventually be a desire for company. Understand it is totally acceptable to cultivate a new relationship after an acceptable time of mourning.

If your spouse was ill for a period of time, you may have begun grieving before the actually passing. In such cases, a year of mourning may be all one needs to arrive at a healthy emotional place. Should the passing be sudden or traumatic, it can take two or three years (or longer) to adequately deal with the grief. If the desire arises, a romance can begin as soon as your heart is whole. Again, the time it takes to heal is unique to the one grieving. It just takes as long as it takes.

Marriage after the Loss of a Child

Marriage is greatly impacted by the loss of a child. The burden of grief can exploit any weakness already existing in the relationship. Though a risk factor, the death of a child does not have to be the beginning of the end for a marriage. Statistics reveal that less than 1 in 5 marriages suffering the death of a child will end in divorce.[1] Couples often pull together and become more tightly knit through the grieving process. *Pulling together* will require four basic practices.

1.   **Communication**. Freely share feelings and emotions with one another. Avoid the marriage killers (blame, anger and resentment)! Give each other license to grieve differently. One spouse may not understand the other's behavior or emotions. Misunderstandings are easily handled by talking through painful emotions.

2.   **Affection**. Affectionate love may feel inappropriate while one is grieving. Physical touch, however, promotes emotional healing.

3.   **Connection**. Draw strength from friends, family, especially others who have shared similar grief. Counseling

may prove very helpful in working through painful emotions.

4. **Action**. Women grieve by feeling, men by doing. Starting again as a couple, will require working together. Some have found great release by building a memorial, or creating a memorial fund. Any activity that honors the life of the child can bring great healing. Taking on a new project or hobby can promote togetherness.

Remember how King David and Bathsheba mourned the loss of their first child. They pulled together and reared Solomon who ushered in the golden era of Israel in the books of 1 Kings and 2 Chronicles. *You can start again.*

Scriptures for further encouragement:

"*But Zion said, 'The Lord has forsaken me, the Lord has forgotten me.' Can a mother forget the baby at her breast and have no compassion on the child she has borne? Though she may forget, I will not forget you! See, I have engraved you on the palms of my hands; your walls are ever before me.*" Isaiah 49:14-16 NIV

"*The LORD is close to the brokenhearted; he rescues those whose spirits are crushed.*" Psalm 34:18 NLT

"*O death, where is your victory? O death, where is your sting?*" 1 Corinthians 15:55 NLT

"*Brothers, we do not want you to be ignorant about those who fall asleep, or to grieve like the rest of men, who have no hope. We believe that Jesus died and rose again and so we believe that God will bring with Jesus those who have fallen asleep in him.*"
1 Thessalonians 4:13-14 NIV

"*I'm leaving you peace. I'm giving you my peace. I don't give you the kind of peace that the world gives. So don't be troubled or cowardly.*" John 14:27 GWT

Chapter 8

A New Beginning in Christ

*"Anyone who belongs to Christ has become a new
person. The old life is gone; a new life has begun."*
2 Corinthians 5:17 NLT

*"The wonder is that Jesus purposed to make
your heart and mine just as sweet and lovely
and pure and holy as His own."*
John G. Lake

No fresh start is as important as the Christ-life.
All other new beginnings will flourish and expire,
at the very latest, with our last breath. The
decision to live by the power of Christ, however,
guarantees the <u>ultimate</u> new beginning in
eternity. While everyone is offered this new start
of heavenly proportions, not all will lay hold of
it. The alterative choice and its consequences are
quite stark.

The Self-Life

One can opt for the self-life. In this path, man
directs his own way, being led by his selfish
desire. The end of this path is pain, regret and

death. Isaiah 53:6 NIV tells us, "*We all, like sheep, have gone astray, each of us has turned to his own way.*" The stray sheep leaves the flock only to wander comfortless and alone. All wayward desires of our heart may seem harmless at first. Proverbs 16:2 warns, "*All a man's ways seem innocent to him, but motives are weighed by the Lord.*" Every choice in life bears fruit that tells the true story. The path of the self-life is littered with broken relationships, failures, emotional pain, forgotten dreams and devastation. Even worse, the self-life shuts the doors of Heaven to us.

Galatians 5:19-21 NLT explains, "*When you follow the desires of your sinful nature, the results are very clear: sexual immorality, impurity, lustful pleasures, idolatry, sorcery, hostility, quarreling, jealousy, outbursts of anger, selfish ambition, dissension, division, envy, drunkenness, wild parties, and other sins like these. Let me tell you again, as I have before, that anyone living that sort of life will not inherit the Kingdom of God.*"

All of us are painfully lost, apart from Christ. The only way to escape the self-life and certain destruction of the soul is to be born again. Jesus declared in John 3:3 NIV, '*I tell you the truth, no one can see the kingdom of God unless he is born again.*'"

Father God sent His Only Son, Jesus, to restore
to us the pathway of eternal life.

> *"God loved the world this way: He gave His only
> Son so that everyone who believes in Him will not
> die but will have eternal life."*
> John 3:16 GWT

> *"This is my Father's will: That everyone who sees
> the Son and believes in Him should have eternal
> life, and I will raise him to life on the last day."*
> John 6:40 ISV

The shed blood of Jesus is the only way to satisfy
the sin-debt of the self-life. Those who reject the
Son for the self-life, also reject the eternal
mercies of the Father. Dear one, *Hell* is filled
with those who refused to choose Christ.

> *"And anyone who believes in God's Son has eternal
> life. Anyone who doesn't obey the Son will never
> experience eternal life but remains under God's
> angry judgment."*
> John 3:36 NLT

> *"Hell hath enlarged herself, and opened her mouth
> without measure: and their glory, and their
> multitude, and their pomp, and he that rejoiceth,
> shall descend into it,"*
> Isaiah 5:14 KJV

The Way of the Cross

Friend, what I'm about to say is of <u>utmost</u> <u>importance</u>. Being *born again* is more than a decision or sinner's prayer. This spiritual rebirth requires inviting the Spirit of the Living God to live within your being. It is permitting Him to create in you the same selfless attitude of His Son Christ. Jesus said in Matthew 16:24, *"If anyone would come after Me, he must deny himself and take up his cross and follow Me."* The way of the new birth is the way of the cross. The cross puts an end to our selfish, sinful ways. Watchman Nee wrote, *"The Blood deals with what we have done, whereas the Cross deals with what we are. The Blood disposes of our sins, while the Cross strikes at the root of our capacity for sin."*

Being *born again* is a work of grace. It cannot be accomplished by mere willpower. Your new birth is of a spiritual nature, not by power or might. This new life is a partnership between Heavenly Father and His newborn son or daughter. Now, He takes over the business of teaching us His ways through His Word, and leading us by His Spirit. How splendidly He helps us in our weakness!

> *"So I say, live by the Spirit, and you will not gratify the desires of the sinful nature."*
> Galatians 5:16 NIV

Beautiful fruit is born from the life lived in unison with God's desires. His desire is that we love one another. "*My command is this: Love each other as I have loved you,*" John 15:12 NIV. This is the way of the cross.

You have not read this book by coincidence! You have been offered the gift of a new life in Christ. By accepting Jesus as your Lord and Savior, you are inviting Him make of you a new creation. Let's pray, together.

Heavenly Father,
Forgive me for living selfishly. My sin and selfish desires have hurt you, others, and myself. I have sinned. Forgive me and give me the power to forgive others who have wronged me, too. I believe in your son, Jesus. Only He could pay my sin-debt. I accept that Christ died on the cross in my place. I ask for your grace. Come live in me, and make of my life a new creation. I choose the way of the cross and the life of love. I choose to daily walk in the spirit.

By Your Spirit, I am born again!
Amen.

Congratulations on your new start! Make certain to begin reading God's Word – His instruction manual for Christian living. The book of St. John is a wonderful place to start. Find a Spirit-filled church home. The pastor and church family will help you find your place in the Body of Christ. The teaching will also ground you in matters of faith. Finally, begin walking in the Spirit. This means doing very spiritual things, like praying, praising God, making melodies in your heart, and sharing His goodness with others. Welcome to the best days of your life!

Endnotes, Chapter 2

1. "National Foreclosure Ticker." *Center for Responsible Lending*. Web. 26 Dec. 2011. <http://www.responsiblelending.org/mortgage-lending/tools-resources/national-foreclosure-ticker.html>.

2. "OCC: New Foreclosures Climb 21.1% in Third Quarter « HousingWire." *HousingWire*. 26 Dec. 2011. <http://www.housingwire.com/2011/12/22/occ-new-foreclosures-climb-21-1>.

3. *American Bankruptcy Institute | Home*. Web. Dec. 2011.<http://www.abiworld.org/AM/AMTemplate.cfm?Section=Home>.

4. Cussen, Mark P. "Top 5 Reasons Why People Go Bankrupt - Yahoo! Finance." *Yahoo! Finance - Business Finance, Stock Market, Quotes, News*. Web. Dec. 2011. <http://finance.yahoo.com/news/pf_article_109143.html>.

Endnotes, Chapter 3

1. "U.S. Underemployment in Mid-December Similar to a Year Ago." *Gallup.Com - Daily News, Polls, Public Opinion on Government, Politics, Economics, Management*. Web. Dec. 2011. <http://www.gallup.com/poll/151601/Underemployment-Mid-December-Similar-Year-Ago.aspx>.

2. National Center for Higher Education Management Systems, "Adding It Up", 2007.

3. Council for Adult and Experiential Learning, "Adult Learner in Focus", 2008.

Endnotes, Chapter 4

1. "Population Profile of the United States." *Census Bureau Homepage*. Web. Dec. 2011. <http://www.census.gov/population/www/pop-profile/geomob.html>.

2. *Ibid*.

Endnotes, Chapter 5

1. Wright, H. Norman. *The Premarital Counseling Handbook*. Singapore: Methodist Book Room, 1992. Print.
2. Ibid, Wright.
3. Ibid, Wright.
4. Ibid, Wright.
5. Ibid, Wright.
6. "U.S. Divorce Rates: for Various Faith Groups, Age Groups and Geographical Areas." *ReligiousTolerance.org*. Web. Dec. 2011. <http://www.religioustolerance.org/chr_dira.htm>.

Endnotes, Chapter 7

1. "Divorce360.com | Divorce and Death of a Child." *Divorce360.com | Divorce Advice, News, Blogs and Community*. Web. Dec. 2011. <http://www.divorce360.com/divorce-articles/causes-of-divorce/general/divorce-and-death-of-a-child.aspx?artid=469>.